Gospel and Ministry :   an Ecumenical Issue

Roman
&
Evangelical

by Per
Erik
Persson

translated by Eric H. Wahlstrom

FORTRESS PRESS   PHILADELPHIA

Translated from *Romerskt och Evangeliskt*
by Per Erik Persson
Gleerups, Lund, 1959

Library of Congress Catalog Card Number 7843664

Printed in U.S.A.   UB974

CONTENTS

I

A NEW SITUATION

Today, no one is likely to deny that in many respects we find ourselves in a new situation in regard to the relationship between the various Christian denominations. More than ever before in history humanity lives both geographically and culturally in *one* world. Distances have been annihilated, and isolation is no longer possible. This applies as well to the churches. They are no longer able to live in their own restricted spheres without paying any attention to the others. The constantly intensified contacts between churches both within and without the World Council of Churches have brought about rapidly expanding conversations across confessional lines.

This new situation prevails not least in regard to the relationship between the Roman Catholic church and the various churches of the Reformation. Ever since the time of the Reformation both

the Lutherans and the Reformed have been compelled to take account of Rome. Now, after centuries
of mutual disregard this dialog has increased in
tempo. A characteristic example of this is the
"Institute for Confessional Research" which was
established by the Lutheran World Federation in
1957, and which is especially concerned with the
relationship between the Lutheran and the Roman
Catholic churches. To be sure, these conversations
have elicited more interest and appear more necessary on the European scene, but there are clear
indications of a similar interest in the United
States among the members of the National Council
of Churches and growing sections of the Roman
Catholic church.

In order that a dialog of this kind might be
fruitful and reach the fundamental levels where
the decisive problems are brought to light, two
conditions must be met. The first is that we earnestly endeavor to understand what the position of
the other member of the dialog really is, and not
what we may think that it is on the basis of
century-old prejudices. The second, which is just
as important, is that we really know what we ourselves stand for and can give reasons for our position. In other words, it is necessary to seek for
greater clarity of both the Roman and the evangelical Protestant positions.

It then becomes initially necessary to remove a
number of common prejudices in regard to the
Roman church and its theology. We must grasp
clearly that the Roman church of today cannot
without further ado be identified with the church

that excluded Luther from its fellowship. The ordinary, religiously oriented Protestant frequently has a ready-made conception of this church, and may describe it in the following general terms.

It is a church which has abandoned the Bible and neglected its study, and which forbids laymen to engage in the study of the Bible on their own initiative. Furthermore it is a church with a petrified order of worship, bound to the Latin language which no one understands. Roman theology is generally regarded as completely dominated by medieval scholasticism with its unintelligible and inaccessible terminology. This theology teaches that man is not saved by God's grace but by his own works. This attitude is seen in the fact that this church bitterly rejected the Reformation and everything that the Reformers had offered to the church on the basis of their discovery of the message of Scripture. And finally it is pointed out that Rome has said an absolute no to the ecumenical movement and stands indifferent to the agonizing problems which confront the church because of its fragmentation into a multiplicity of denominations.

If on the basis of these and similar presuppositions we engage in a study of the Roman Catholic church of today, the encounter with Rome becomes a surprising and confusing experience. We will be compelled to revise our conception on one point after another.

In the first place, we have to revise our opinion about the place of the *Bible* within the Roman Catholic church. The Bible has not at all been set aside and it is no longer difficult to obtain. We find one translation after another in the various languages, very often in inexpensive editions prepared for mass distribution. Many of these translations are of superior quality, both in fidelity to the original text and in literary excellence. It is no exaggeration to say that in the Roman Catholic church of today we find a biblical revival of great extent and importance. The reading of the Bible by laymen is greatly encouraged, although restricted of course to translations approved by the church. To help the laymen in this study there is a constantly growing supply of outlines for Bible study, lexicons and brief commentaries on the various books of the Bible.

Closely related to this development and possibly one of its main causes is a rapidly increasing interest in scholarly exegesis, which is now encouraged and promoted even by the highest authorities. The most important document in this area was the remarkable papal encyclical of 1943 *Divino afflante Spiritu*. In this message Pius XII emphasized among other things that the object of scholarly research must first of all be the original Hebrew and Greek texts, which have superior authority over every translation, including even the Vulgate which is the official Latin text of the Roman church.[1] We can safely say that today Roman Catholic exegesis, after a troubled start, has as a whole appropriated the historical-critical method and has made a very valuable contribution

[1] *Divino afflante Spiritu*, in Henry Denzinger *The Sources of Catholic Dogma*, trans. Roy J. Deferrari (St. Louis: B. Herder, 1957), p. 620.

to the work of textual criticism.

In recent years there have appeared a number of thorough and profound works in purely biblical theology, which is really a new development. During the first session of the Second Vatican Council (1962), the strong position of this new work appeared clearly in the unexpected opposition that greeted the proposal put forth by the conservative element in the Curia for a decision by the Council in regard to "the sources of revelation." This proposal was returned to a commission for revision, and not the least reason for this action was the fact that the proposal would have put a stop to the new biblical research. The present situation, then, is this: exegesis to a greater extent than any other theological discipline is a common field where confessional boundaries no longer obtain, and where the results achieved become the property of all. It remains true, however, that in his work the Roman exegete has to follow the guidelines which are given in the teaching tradition of his own church. Protestants sometimes fail to take this factor into account, and therefore tend to accept uncritically the results of Roman Catholic exegesis.

In the second place, when we consider the *worship life* of the Roman church we must realize that the use of the Latin language, which is difficult for us to understand, has a very positive meaning for the faithful Roman. Wherever he goes in the world, he finds the same liturgy and the same Latin language as in his home parish. The Mass thus becomes a bond which units all the Roman

Catholics of the Western rite just as effectively as obedience to the Pope. Yet at this point we can now expect rather extensive reforms. According to the liturgical proposal adopted at the second session of the Second Vatican Council (1963), it will be possible by decision of the regional bishop conferences to celebrate the greater part of the Mass in the language of the people.

Another expression of the lively liturgical renewal within the Roman Catholic church is the new emphasis on the function of the sermon in the Mass. According to the Council the first part of the Mass with its center in the reading of Scripture and the delivery of the sermon, and the latter part consisting in the sacrifice of the Mass, are "of equal importance" to the believer. In connection with this renaissance of the sermon in worship we find an increasing endeavor to secure a greater participation on the part of laymen in the worship in order to make the Mass a real congregational service of worship. It would seem, however, that "the private Mass" without any congregation present will remain as a legitimate worship practice. In comparison with the demands of the Reformers it is interesting to note that a possibility has been granted where the laymen, under certain circumstances, as for example at an Ordination Mass, may also receive the cup. When this happens the practice of the Latin rite since the thirteenth century has in principle been broken. We may mention other liturgical reforms adopted before the meeting of the Council, such as the radical changes in the liturgy of Holy Week and

Easter, and the concessions in regard to fasting which have made it possible to celebrate the Mass with communion in the evening.

In the third place, as we turn to a consideration of the *theology* of the church in the strict sense we find no trace of the common Protestant assumption that the Roman church teaches that salvation is by good works rather than by the grace of God. On the contrary, it is taught very clearly that man's salvation is possible only on the basis of the grace of God. At the same time, however, it is clear that "grace" does not here have exactly the same connotation as in the Protestant theological tradition. As a matter of fact, that salvation is possible only by God's grace means that it is by God's grace alone that the good and meritorious works which are necessary for salvation become possible. In this way, to be sure, the absolute necessity of grace is emphasized, but it is not understood as in Reformation theology as something that absolutely excludes all consideration of human merit. On the contrary, grace is precisely the necessary condition for meritorious action.

Even in the area of theology we note moreover some movement toward reform. In addition to what we have already observed in the area of exegesis we find that research in the history of dogma has shifted in emphasis from scholasticism to the church fathers of the first centuries. In the area of patristics the Roman Catholic scholars are currently undoubtedly in the lead. This factor also tends to influence the strictly dogmatic works. As we compare the older and the newer dogmatic

works, we find in the latter a well-defined tendency
to reject the scholastic conceptual scheme. Instead
they seek to use a terminology influenced by biblical theology and patristics. What this development means can easily be seen in a comparison
between a traditional Roman Catholic catechism
as, for example, *The Baltimore Catechism*,[2] and
the new German common catechism, which, after
its tremendous popularity in continental Europe,
is now also available in the United States under
the title *The Living Faith*.[3] It is interesting to note
that this change in regard to terminology and presentation has taken place in accordance with the
clearly stated intention to serve more adequately
the task of the church in proclaiming the Christian
message to modern man. The intensive work in
biblical studies which we have noted above is thus
bearing fruit in all areas of theology. It is significant that in the encyclical *Mystici Corporis
Christi* (1943), which until the Second Vatican
Council constituted the fundamental document for
the modern Roman Catholic doctrine of the church,
Pius XII worked with a characteristic Pauline
theme, namely, the church as the body of Christ.[4]
Moreover, in the coming decree on "The Church,"
thoroughly discussed during the second session of
the Council, the biblical idea of the church as the

[2] Francis J. Connell, *Baltimore Catechism No. 3* (Confra-
ternity Ed.; New York: Benziger Brothers, 1952).

[3] *The Living Faith,* adapted by Gerard Floyan from the
German *Katholische Katechismus* (New York: Herder and
Herder, 1959).

[4] *Mystici Corporis Christi,* in *The Church Teaches: Documents of the Church in English Translation,* ed. John F.
Clarkson, *et al.* (St. Louis: B. Herder, 1955), pp. 107-18.

people of God will play a central role. Another conspicuous fact is that theology is more and more concerned with the previously neglected task of clarifying and defining the vocation of the laymen as a necessary and active part of the church as a whole.

In the fourth place, we can also observe a striking change in the Roman Catholic evaluation of the *Reformation* and its theology. In works of church history we find a radical re-examination of the event of the Reformation which has resulted in a frequently expressed recognition that the blame for the unfortunate schism in the church must not be placed unilaterally on the Reformers. Furthermore, we now find a completely new and positive appreciation of Luther's theological intentions, which formerly was totally absent. Within Roman Catholicism today, moreover, there are theological works which discuss the Reformation as a problem *within* the church, a problem with which the church always has to deal. The title of a work by a German theologian is significant: "The Reformation as a Contemporary Religious Concern."[5] Many Roman Catholic theologians and even some of the hierarchy now clearly express their antipathy toward the theology that was determined by the conflicts of the Counter Reformation and has prevailed up to the present time. Not least, the two first sessions of the Second Vatican Council have manifested a will toward reform which comes as a surprise to many. The old for-

[5] Joseph Lortz, *Die Reformation als religiöses Anliegen heute* (Trier, 1948).

mula *ecclesia semper reformanda* is no longer a Protestant prerogative, but expresses something that belongs to the nature of the church even from the Roman Catholic point of view.

In the fifth place, it is well known that Rome officially declines to participate in the *ecumenical endeavors* which have found their principal organizational expression in the World Council of Churches. The reason for this is of course that Rome sees the unity of the church of Christ realized in principle in its own church, and consequently any striving for Christian unity must, strictly speaking, mean a return to Rome. But this does not at all prevent Roman Catholics from following the ecumenical movement with great interest. At the great ecumenical conferences they are represented by official observers. There are a number of periodicals whose principal purpose is to inform their readers about the ecumenical debates outside their own church. There are several excellent books by Roman Catholics dealing with the origin and history of the ecumenical movement. But the strongest evidence of a change in the area of ecumenicity is found in what has happened in connection with the Second Vatican Council. The preparation for the Council included even the establishment of a "Secretariat for Christian Unity" to serve as a point of contact between the Roman Catholic church and other churches. There is no precedent for this action in the history of previous councils. Through this secretariat a number of observers were invited to the Council from both the World Council of Churches and other church groups. These observers have not only had the opportunity to follow the discussions but have also been provided with copies of the strictly confidential documents which serve as the basis for these discussions. Through direct contact with the members of the Council the reactions of these observers have found expression even in the discussions of the Council itself.

These examples, here presented only very briefly, show clearly that the Roman Catholic church today appears especially in its theology rather perplexing. We find a number of features on which we in the past have claimed monopoly. There appears a rediscovery of the church fathers and of Scripture in connection with a liturgical renewal which on many points seeks to realize the original intentions of the Reformers.

But it is not only in Rome that we find such changes as to enable us without hesitation to say that the relationship between the churches has come into a new situation. In the Protestant churches, Lutheran as well as Reformed, we find at the same time a rediscovery of the doctrine of the church. The problems connected with the concepts of "church," "sacrament," and "ministry" are today almost everywhere found in the center of theological discussion. Likewise there is in Protestant theology today an entirely new appreciation of the place of tradition in the church. The new situation has been described very pointedly by Robert McAfee Brown: "What is happening now is that Catholic theology is restoring to Scripture a place of greater significance, while Protestant theology is really beginning to take seriously the extent to which contemporary understanding of Scripture is moulded and conditioned by tradition."[6]

We find ourselves therefore in a new and previously untried situation in regard to the relationship between the denominations. At first glance it appears that the lines of demarcation which formerly seemed so definite and distinct no longer run parallel but tend more and more to converge. Especially in the areas of exegetical and patristic theology do the confessional lines appear to a great extent obliterated. In these areas Protestant and Roman Catholic scholars work side by side and gratefully share suggestions and points of view. But even in works on systematic theology scholars on both sides often seem to use the same language and the same expressions. It is obvious that the old, cherished criteria can no longer be applied without some revision.

These changes do not make the task of trying to see where the decisive differences lie any less necessary than before, rather they make this task more imperative than ever. These lines of demarcation are still there, even if they are at first more difficult to discover now that scholars on both sides of the confessional boundaries seem frequently to be saying the same things. Furthermore, the task assumes greater reality when our view is no longer obscured by tenaciously persistent and in the last analysis false clichés. It is clear that

[6] Robert M. Brown and Gustave Weigel, *An American Dialogue: A Protestant Looks at Catholicism and a Catholic Looks at Protestantism* (New York: Doubleday, 1960), p. 88.

we no longer gain anything by speaking about the Roman Catholic church as "a stranger to the Bible," and in the same context the Roman Catholic cannot say to us that we do not know anything about "the church." The line no longer runs between a theology in which there is much said about the Bible but little about the church and the tradition, and another theology that says a great deal about the church and tradition but little about the Bible. The situation is now that these subjects are the center of attention on all sides. It is no longer a question about "more" or "less," but the fundamental question is *how* each side understands Scripture and tradition and their mutual relationship. In this new situation, where the points of interest seem to converge, we must not break off the conversation or refrain from asking the fundamental questions about the lines of demarcation between Roman Catholic and evangelical Protestant points of view. Even now, as once in the sixteenth century, the fundamental question concerns the very nature of the gospel.

When in the following pages of this book we assume the task of clarifying and analyzing the problems here indicated, it becomes necessary to limit the discussion to some decisive points and conceptions. Limitations of space compel us to concentrate on those questions which today occupy the central place in the discussions within both Protestant and Roman Catholic theology. In other words, we are concerned here with the problems which have a direct relationship to the conceptions of "the word" and "the church."

II

SCRIPTURE AND THE CHURCH

A Common Objective?

In evangelical theology and church life during recent decades we find a growing appreciation of the place of the sacraments in the church. In a unique way this "sacramental" development in Protestantism has a counterpart in Roman Catholic circles in a manifest renaissance of the study of the Bible and a corresponding endeavor to give the proclamation of the word a prominent place in the worship life of the church.

If we consider the Reformation, it is clear that the very preaching of the word occupied there a central and decisive place. The renewal of the church in the Reformation involved not least a renewal of preaching. Martin Luther made his Reformation discovery of the righteousness from God through faith in Christ while he struggled with the text of the Bible; and that joyous message which he found to be the chief content of

Scripture had to be conveyed and made known to men. In this sense the word of preaching was not conceived of as information or instruction about something that had happened, or was about to happen, but it was understood as something through which Christ himself, incarnate, crucified and risen, now comes to those who hear in order to give himself, his righteousness and his life to them. The sermon was not a communication of doctrine. On the contrary, the word proclaimed as law and gospel represented an activity that brings salvation: judgment on sin and self-righteousness, and a bestowal of that forgiveness which, as a word from God, possessed a life-giving and recreating power. The word of preaching was the living word of the gospel in the present, *viva vox*.[1]

In recent Roman Catholic theology we often find expressions that are surprisingly similar to the vocabulary of the Reformation. The Pauline word that "faith comes from preaching" is emphasized again and again. The earlier, common view that the sermon was a communication of doctrine, which was focused on the sacraments and was designed to prepare men for the reception of that salvation which the sacraments mediate, is now regarded as a heresy that originated in the rationalism of the Enlightenment, but which is now being overcome both in theology and practice. Against the background of exegetical investigations of the biblical idea of the word of God as a creative and active word, the word of preaching, *viva vox*, is now defined as "an audible sacrament,"

[1] See H. Ivarsson, *Predikans uppgift* (Lund, 1956), pp. 19 ff.

on the analogy of Augustine's well-known statement about the sacraments as "a visible word."
Since the church is an extension of the incarnate
word, preaching belongs to the very nature of the
church, and if the church should neglect this task,
it would prove false to itself and to its commission
in the world.[2] We find statements of this sort, not
only among reckless vanguards who might be
suspected of being influenced by Protestant theology, but also in statements by the highest and
most authoritative persons. Thus Pope Pius XII,
in a speech delivered at the meeting of the General Chapter of the Dominican Order (1946), said
that the preacher does not only present words about
Christ to his listeners, but, just as once the Virgin
Mary did, so he presents and gives to them Jesus
Christ himself. He is *Christopher*, a bearer of Christ.

In view of these statements, we can understand
that many are beginning to ask whether we do
not here encounter a common objective. Obviously
it is no longer possible in the present situation to
resort to the habitual clichés, "the church of the
sacraments" and "the church of the word," in
order to designate the Roman and the evangelical
positions. Would we not have good reason for
abandoning the old confessional quarrel when our
opponents begin to speak our own language? Yet,
in spite of all this, it is still true that a decisive
line of demarcation runs right through the statements which now seem to bear witness to a mutual

[2] M. Schmaus, *Katholische Dogmatik* III: 1 (Munich, 1958),
pp. 786 ff., the section on *Heilshaftigkeit der Wortverkün-
dung*.

objective. This becomes clear when in this connection we seek for an answer to two decisive
questions: What is the content of the church's
proclamation today? and, What is the basis for the
thesis—as held by the respective parties—that the
proclamation is a living and life-giving word?

Scripture, Tradition, and the Teaching Office

If we direct the first of the above questions to
the Reformers, we receive an answer which is
virtually self-evident. The proclamation in the
present must both be derived from and further
extend that word of God which is found in Holy
Scripture. That gospel about Christ, which the
apostles once proclaimed, and which "grew and
prevailed mightily" in the early church (Acts
19:20), is to be proclaimed today by those who
have been entrusted with this commission. Just
as the apostolic proclamation was an exposition
of Holy Scripture, what we today call the Old
Testament, so the function of the present-day sermon is to expound Holy Scripture, the writings of
both the Old and the New Covenants, which now
share a common witness to Christ. The Bible is
not primarily conceived of as a "book," an entity
sufficient unto itself, but as a message from God
to men, and for this reason its content must continually be directed anew to succeeding generations
of men in the form of a proclamation. The word
which is now proclaimed is itself the word of God
because it expresses that "fact" to which the whole
Bible bears witness, viz., God's act of redemption
through Christ. The dependence of the sermon on

the biblical text is in the last analysis an indication of the fact that it is exactly this message as contained in the Bible, and nothing else, that is to be set forth even now. When this is done, the gospel derived from Scripture is still a living and active word, "the power of God for salvation to every one who has faith" (Rom. 1:16).

If we then direct our question about the content of the church's proclamation and teaching to the Roman theology, we receive an answer of a different kind. Not that they would speak depreciatingly about Scripture. On the contrary, they speak frequently about Scripture and quote Bible passages diligently, not least in recent dogmatic works, and they frequently and strongly emphasize the character of the Bible as the word of God. Roman theology prides itself, and in one sense rightly, on the fact that it better than anyone else incisively maintained the authoritative position of the Bible, its infallibility and divine inspiration, during the so-called liberal period, which in Roman Catholic terminology is referred to as "Modernism." It was the Council of Trent, and not the Reformers, which finally, in 1546, determined the extent of the biblical canon; and the Vatican Council, the same Council that in 1870 established the dogma of the infallibility of the Pope, emphasized that the church adheres to the biblical writing as holy and canonical, not because she guarantees them by her own authority, but because they are written under the inspiration of the Holy Spirit, and therefore have God himself as their ultimate author. Scripture contains the revealed, divine truth, which the church must set forth in its proclamation, and this revelation was finished with the death of the last apostle. But, and here is the decisive point, this does not mean that Scripture contains the *whole* revealed truth; in any case, it is not to be found there in the complete form in which it appears in the doctrinal teaching of the church today.

In order correctly to understand the present problem on this point we must resort to a brief review of historical developments. It is sometimes said in a rather misleading formulation that the evangelical churches represent the principle of Scripture, "Scripture alone," while the Roman church is known for its tendency to speak of "Scripture *and* tradition." This simplified formula is misleading because there is no church and no theology that does not live in a tradition. A specific doctrinal tradition is not found only in Roman circles, and we may with the same appropriateness speak of a "Lutheran," a "Reformed," or an "Anglican" tradition. The difference is not between those who maintain Scripture alone and those who add tradition, but the question is rather how we understand the latter entity in its relationship to the former. It is at this point that the paths diverge.

When the fathers in the ancient church appeal to the apostolic tradition against the alleged, secretly preserved, special tradition of the Gnostics, they appeal to the testimony of Scripture. We find here a peculiarly self-evident unity between the principles of tradition and Scripture. The same idea appears in the theology of the Middle Ages, where the teaching tradition of the church is conceived of primarily as *interpretative*; it is nothing else than the continuous exposition of Scripture in the church. In this case the Scripture principle is the self-evident presupposition for the theological task. The proclamation and instruction of the church is understood as an exposition of the content of Holy Scripture.

But if this is the case (and this is something which we ought to pay attention to in our own discussions within the church), it becomes obvious that this very Scripture principle as such is not something that is especially characteristic of the Reformation. Both those theologians who were loyal to the Pope, and the spiritualist movements, which Luther so earnestly opposed, appealed to the Bible. What was new in Luther was not "Scripture alone," but that he on the basis of that principle, which was more or less accepted by all, violently attacked the accepted contemporary interpretation of Scripture. Luther did this on the basis of what during the nineteenth century came to be called the "material" principle of the Reformation, "justification by faith alone," which he had actually derived from Scripture ("the formal principle"). We never discover what is really unique in the Reformation as long as we talk only about "Scripture alone." The meaning of this formula can be found only in an indissoluble unity between the "formal" and the "material" principles. If "the formal principle" is separated from this unity, we are no longer dealing with the *Lutheran* principle of Scripture, but with a general Christian principle on the basis of which almost

anything may be validated. It is significant that
the Lutheran confessional writings do not contain
a completely developed doctrine of Scripture as
such, but that we find there an argumentation for
justification through faith in Christ supported point
by point with citations from biblical texts. *This*
kind of biblically-supported argumentation is what
is typical of the Reformation; but on the basis of
this use of Scripture, the Bible itself came to appear
as a critical authority over against the prevalent
doctrinal development, and thereby a new situation was created. The earlier, self-evident unity
between Scripture and the teaching of the church
was challenged.

In this situation it was necessary for the Council
of Trent, whose assignment it was to define and
establish the Roman position in this crisis, to consider the problem of Scripture and its interpretation as one of its very first tasks. The members of
the Council emphasized very strongly that under
no circumstances was it permissible to interpret
Scripture contrary to the teaching of the church,
*contra eum sensum, quem tenuit et tenet sancta
mater Ecclesia*, a formula which continually appears in later official documents. But in order to
be able to preserve the traditional teaching of the
church, they made a decision which became decisive for the later development, viz., to place the
apostolic tradition, the original oral tradition which
had lived on in the church and was to be found
in the writings of the fathers, by the side of Scripture as a source of revelation on a par with that
same Scripture. According to the Council of Trent

we find the revealed and saving truth in the books of Scripture *and* in the unwritten traditions preserved by the church.

During the following centuries this "and" was interpreted to mean that Scripture contains only a part of the original revelation. The truth delivered to the church was found *partly* in Scripture and *partly* in tradition. But by this development we have been presented with a new conception of tradition contrary to that previously held. The tradition is now no longer an interpretation of Scripture but a *complement* to it. Furthermore, this complementary tradition was conceived of as something relatively static, a body of truths of faith once for all given, the content of which was essentially the same in the seventeenth century as in the days of the apostles.

Even if we can support this view by adducing examples from one or more older textbooks, this conception does not constitute the principal line of thought in Roman theology today. During the nineteenth century a new development took place. The stimulus came from the celebrated Tübingen school of theology in Germany, where such men as J. A. Möhler and M. J. Scheeben were lecturing, and perhaps not least from Cardinal Newman, who currently is the object of much interest in Roman Catholic theology. Briefly, this new point of view means that the older, static interpretation of the tradition has been replaced by a more living and dynamic conception. "Scripture" and "tradition" are no longer regarded as two independent entities in relation to one another, but the two coalesce

in the dynamic unity of the *church* as it develops
through the centuries. It is no longer simply a
question of preserving what has once for all been
given to the church, but now the Roman theologians speak also of developing to a greater degree
of clarity that which from the beginning was only
suggestively present in the revelation. They are
beginning to speak of the church and its consciousness of faith as an organism, which has grown from
the small beginning in the seed to an ever greater
perfection and profusion. Scripture and the older
tradition, as the original datum, surely contain the
saving truth, but not to the full and ample extent
in which it today appears in the church.

We must be fully aware of the fact that it is
not a question here of "a continuing revelation."
Revelation was closed with the death of the last
apostle, and what is asserted is only that the church
through the centuries has gradually obtained a
deeper and clearer insight into the meaning of
that which was once for all given. This has
happened and does continually happen through
"the living tradition" of the church, i.e., the
church's constantly developing consciousness of
faith. On this basis we may in one sense say that
Roman theology has returned to the conception of
the tradition as an interpretation by the church
of the given revelation which was prevalent in the
ancient church and in the Middle Ages. As a result of this it is possible to combine the present
proclamation of the church with Scripture in an
entirely different way than heretofore. The revelation contained in the biblical writings no longer

stands as a static entity by the side of the tradition of the church, but this revelation is now found *in* this tradition itself, made alive in the proclamation of the church. It is in this context that we find statements about *viva vox*.

Yet, between the Middle Ages and the church in the present stands the decision of the Council of Trent, and consequently the current interpretation of the concept of tradition does differ decisively from that which was prevalent in the ancient church and among the scholastic theologians. The task of the church is indeed to interpret and expound the word of God given in revelation, but this word is found now not only in Scripture but *also* in the tradition. It is primarily to this living voice of tradition that we must turn in order to find an answer to the question of the content of that message which the church has been commissioned to proclaim.

In one sense, therefore, the tie to Scripture and to the oldest witness of the tradition is broken. The criterion for the correctness of a doctrine no longer consists in the fact that the doctrine can be found clearly expressed in the canonical writings or in the fathers, but in that it is actually found in the church today, i.e., that it is sanctioned by the teaching ministry of the church. At the same time the dependence on Scripture and on the oldest tradition is maintained by the insistence that what today is clearly and plainly taught in the church must be assumed to be present in the oldest documents, at least in allusions, or in a germinal state. If at this point some difficulties should arise, this does not constitute a decisive objection against what is now being taught in the church, because the legitimacy of what is being taught is given directly in and through its being actually, presently taught. One Roman Catholic dogmatist has expressed this in a characteristic formulation: "The legitimacy of a doctrinal decision of the church lies in its facticity."[3] The "correctness" of a doctrinal decision is not dependent on whether "proofs" can be deduced from Scripture or the tradition, for it has this correctness in itself, *der Grund ihrer Richtigkeit in sich selbst.*[4]

Unity and continuity with the time of the founding of the church is not guaranteed by a conformity with the prophetic and apostolic message found in Scripture. The guarantee lies in the fact that it is one and the same living organism which has been developed from the earliest time of the church into the present. From this point of view it would be just as absurd to demand conformity between the faith of the ancient church and the church of today as to insist that the fully-developed tree with trunk and crown and all should be present already in the seed. The conception of an organism makes it possible, on the one hand, to hold firmly that the revelation has been given once for all and was finished at the death of the last apostle (which of course excludes the idea that a *new* truth could in any real sense

---

[3] *In der Fakticität einer kirchlichen Lehrentscheidung liegt ihre Legitimität.* M. Schmaus, *op. cit.*, III: 1, p. 811.

[4] *Ibid.*

be revealed later), and, on the other hand, to speak about the growing insight of the church into the revealed truth, an insight which permits the formulation of doctrinal statements which were unknown to or even rejected by earlier generations in the church.

It might in a sense be correct to say that when it was a question of guaranteeing the correctness and legitimacy of the church's prevailing inter- pretation of revelation, the decisive element before Trent was the proof from Scripture, and after Trent the additional proof from tradition (in the sense of a series of historically authenticated statements handed down from the ancient time of the church). But now it is neither Scripture nor tradition (in the older meaning), but the church's current con- sciousness of faith, incarnate in the teaching office of the church, which is the primary criterion of truth. What this teaching office, which alone in its infallibility is able to decide the correct mean- ing of both Scripture and tradition, now proclaims is thereby also the true content of revelation.

Roman Catholic theology maintains just as in- tensively as the Reformers once did that the living proclamation of the church now has the task to bring forth correctly that which was contained in the original revelation, that and nothing else. But in the very center of this thesis there is an un- bridgeable gulf between the two parties. This gulf is reflected in the content of the doctrines but in the last analysis depends on the criterion by which each side determines the identity between the present proclamation of the church and the gospel

which Jesus himself and his apostles preached.
Here the Reformers, and after them all evangelical
theology, demand a conformity to Scripture, while
Roman theology just as clearly demands a conformity to the teaching ministry of the church.
This conception is clearly expressed in the thesis,
which commonly appears in Roman Catholic dogmatic presentations and has been sharply emphasized in Pope Pius XII's encyclical *Humani generis*
(1950), namely, that the teaching office is the
primary canon of faith, *regula proxima fidei*, while
Scripture and tradition as *regula fidei remota* serve
only in a secondary capacity as a norm for the
content of faith. This does not at all mean that
these latter two cease to be normative, but that
they are normative only in the sense defined by
the teaching office.[5]

This posture becomes immediately significant
for the conception of the nature and purpose of
the theological task. While in evangelical circles
the question of "correct doctrine" is decided by
reference to the exposition of biblical texts, the
Roman theologian is directed primarily to the
statements by the teaching office. The teaching
office of the church, not the content of Scripture
or the testimony of tradition, is the primary source
for the content both of the individual's faith and
of the theologian's intense effort to clarify this
content of faith. "The church in its living teaching
office is the immediate and proximate source of
faith and at the same time of the theological study
of the faith, while Scripture and tradition are the

[5] *Humani generis*, in Denzinger, *op. cit.*, pp. 635-47.

remote rule of faith."[6] The theologian's scholarly research into available historical texts and testimonies of faith may well serve to provide advice and instruction, but it has no decisive relevance for the final formulation of the content of the Christian faith. This does not mean, however, that the study of the textual sources has no significance, or that theology has no task to perform, or that it is limited to areas where the teaching office has not yet spoken the decisive word. When a point of doctrine has been finally validated by this office, "the most noble function of theology is to show how a doctrine defined by the church is contained in the sources" (i.e., Scripture and tradition). This statement is taken from Pope Pius XII's encyclical *Humani generis* (1950), and delimits the phrase "defined by the church" by quoting Pope Pius IX: "By that very sense by which it is defined."[7] This encyclical of Pius XII also rejects the idea, suggested by some, that the significance of the newer decisions promulgated by the teaching office ought to be interpreted on the basis of the ancient sources and the writings of the fathers. On the contrary, it is these latter that are to be interpreted on the basis of what the church declares today.

[6] *Die Kirche ist in ihrem lebendigen Lehramt die unmittelbare und nächste Quelle des Glaubens und damit der Glaubenswissenschaft, während Schrift und Tradition die "entfernte Glaubensregel" sind.* M. Schmaus, *Katholische Dogmatik* I (Munich, 1940), p. 32.

[7] *Humani generis*, in Denzinger, *op. cit.*, p. 641. The quotation from Pius IX is from his encyclical of 1870 *Inter gravissimas.*

New Dogmas

The history of Roman Catholic theology during the last century is characterized by a formulation of dogmas, which depends upon the development outlined above, and which has no counterpart within other churches. A brief review of the origin and significance of these dogmas may clarify better than any theoretical treatment what this view of the relationship between "the word and the church" concretely signifies.

The growing importance which has come to be assigned to the teaching office of the church found tangible expression in the dogma of *the infallibility of the Pope*, proclaimed by Pope Pius IX at the First Vatican Council (1870). This dogma does not imply that the Pope is "sinless," for as every other Roman Catholic he has a father confessor, nor that he might not err in personal affairs. But it does mean that the Pope by virtue of divine assistance is infallible when he solemnly, *ex cathedra*, issues a decision which is binding on the whole church in reference to the faith or the Christian life. He possesses this infallibility by virtue of his office, *ex sese*, and this is not dependent on a prior consent of the church, i.e., a church council. Roman theologians disagree about the extent to which this infallibility may also be attributed to other papal pronouncements on questions of doctrine. This situation is due to the fact that neither at the First Vatican Council nor later has it been perfectly clear under what circumstances a statement has been unmistakably made *ex ca-*

thedra. Pius XII, however, in *Humani generis* rejected the occasionally-expressed idea that one must accept unequivocally what has been solemnly defined *ex cathedra*, but may disregard the more regularly issued papal encyclicals.[8]

The concentration of this dogmatic authority in the papal office had in a sense been anticipated in 1854, when Pius IX without a previous decision of a church council proclaimed the dogma of *the immaculate conception of the Virgin Mary*. This dogma means in brief that Mary from the time of her conception was by divine intervention free from sin in every form during every moment of her life. The latest Marian dogma too, *assumptio Mariae*, the Virgin Mary's assumption into heaven, was declared in 1950 without the consent of a previous church council.

The circumstances of the origin of these two Marian dogmas, which every faithful Roman Catholic must believe and hold to as firmly as, for instance, the dogmas of creation and incarnation, are of special interest at this point in our discussion. Earlier in history, after the schism between the Eastern and the Western churches, decisions in respect to points of doctrine were made at a church council called and presided over by the Pope, and always in a situation marked by a difference of opinion in regard to the meaning of a certain point of doctrine. Different opinions had been expressed, and a decision had to be made to determine the correct teaching. This was the case, for instance, in respect to the dogma of transub-

[8] *Ibid.*, p. 640.

stantiation during the Middle Ages, and in respect to the decree of the Council of Trent aimed at the Reformers' doctrine of justification. In regard to the more recent Marian dogmas the situation is different, because here we have the church's own present and uncontested consciousness of faith promulgated as dogma.

Furthermore, we encounter a new basis for the contention that the dogma to be defined is found also in the revelation once for all entrusted to the church, *depositum fidei*. In earlier times it was held that proofs must be found both in Scripture and tradition, the latter in the form of a series of consistent statements by the fathers which could be historically validated. But before the promulgation of the dogma of the immaculate conception of the Virgin Mary the theological commission appointed by the Pope declared that a point of doctrine can be defined as revealed truth even though Scripture yields no direct testimony to it; consequently the definition can be on the basis of tradition alone. The decisive question then becomes what in this connection is meant by "tradition." In regard to this it is further explained that the presence of this tradition is demonstrated if one is able to show an actually present consensus in the church *no matter at what time this consensus is found.*

The most interesting example of this development is found, however, in the promulgation in 1950 of the latest Marian dogma, that of the Virgin's bodily assumption into heaven. The Roman

Catholic scholar Berthold Altaner, one of the leading authorities on patristics in our generation, pointed out in a notable series of articles *before* the proclamation of the dogma, that there is no scriptural proof for this dogma, nor is there in the strict sense any evidence for it in tradition.[9] The idea of Mary's assumption into heaven appears actually to be completely unknown during the first four centuries; there are, rather, a number of examples of the expectation that Mary was included among those who are to rise on the last day. The idea of the assumption appears first in the fifth century in a legend of Gnostic origin, which has been adorned with many fantastic features. It is known under the title *Transitus Mariae*. It was judged apocryphal by the Roman church of that time and was included in a list of forbidden books, which is found in the so-called *Decretum Gelasianum* from the sixth century.

Altaner regards the *Transitus* legend as a product of pure fantasy, a special example of the growing collection of martyr legends from that time. Only in the seventh century do we find what may be called a beginning of a theological reflection on the basis of the *Transitus* legend. But, as Altaner points out, a pious legend is and remains a legend, and its claim to truth does not become greater just because more and more people begin to believe it. The reference to the present faith of the church

[9] Berthold Altaner, "Zur Frage der Definibilität der *Assumptio Beatae Mariae Virginis*," *Theologische Revue*, XLIV (1948), cols. 129-40; XLV (1949), cols. 129-42; XLVI (1950), cols. 5-20.

becomes in reality only circular reasoning without conclusive proof: a certain belief for which no usually acceptable theological evidence can be found arises in the church, and then the very existence of this belief is cited as evidence for its validity. It is characteristic, however, that Altaner, after making these very emphatic statements, nevertheless cautiously declares that *if* it should happen that the teaching office of the church should affirm that the idea of Mary's assumption into heaven is not only a pious opinion but a divinely revealed truth, the theologian must admit that the Holy Spirit through his assistance to the teaching office has conveyed and clarified something which could not have been attained and established on the basis of the scholarly study of the available texts.

This hesitation in regard to a definition of dogma, as expressed by Altaner and many others, had in this specific instance no effect. The most compelling factor was the popular piety as deeply rooted in the practice of the church, together with Pius XII's strong and frequently expressed interest in Mariology. From the time of 1861 onward a constantly growing number of petitions were addressed to the Curia asking for a promulgation of the doctrine. It is estimated that the petitions had a total of thirteen million signatures. To a papal questionnaire addressed in 1946 to all the bishops, asking whether they thought a promulgation of the dogma possible and opportune, the affirmative answers were 98 percent, and only 1.8 percent expressed any reservations.

But this does not mean that the dogma was based *only* on the actually existing consensus of faith in the church. In the apostolic constitution *Munificentissimus Deus*, in which the *Assumption of Mary* was proclaimed, we find that this dogma is based also on Scripture as the ultimate ground, *ultimum fundamentum*. In Scripture Mary appears in a most intimate relationship to her Son. She always shares in his life, and therefore it would appear impossible that after his death she would be physically separated from him. This reasoning on the basis of the so-called convenience proof is extremely characteristic. "And, since He (Christ) could adorn her with so great a gift as to keep her unharmed by the corruption of the tomb, it must be believed that He actually did this."[10] The argument runs along the following line: it is possible for God to act in a certain way, it is also exceedingly appropriate and fitting for him to do so, therefore he has done it.

On the first of November, 1950, the new dogma was solemnly proclaimed by Pius XII from the Plaza of St. Peter in Rome. ". . . by the authority of our Lord Jesus Christ, of the Blessed Apostles, Peter and Paul, and by Our own authority We pronounce, declare, and define that the dogma was revealed by God, that the Immaculate Mother of God, the ever Virgin Mary, after completing her course of life upon earth, was assumed to the glory of heaven both in body and soul. Therefore, if

[10] *Munificentissimus Deus*, in Denzinger, *op. cit.*, p. 647.

anyone, which may God forbid, should dare either
to deny this, or voluntarily call into doubt what
has been defined by Us, he should realize that he
has cut himself off entirely from the divine and
Catholic faith."[11]

[11] *Ibid.*, p. 648.

III

THE LIVING WORD

We now proceed to the question of the bases on which both sides advance the thesis that the church's proclamation is a living and life-giving word. We may find a suitable point of departure in the words about the Holy Spirit as "the Lord and Giver of life" as found in the Nicene Creed which is common to both the Roman Catholic and the evangelical Lutheran churches. The consideration will deal with the way each side understands the work of the Spirit in the church. That to which the active presence of the Spirit is attached will thereby also appear as the constitutive and creative element for the church, that spring out of which life and salvation flow.

The Spirit and the Word

If we approach the classical documents of the Lutheran Reformation, as they are found in that church's confessional writings, and ask the question about the Spirit and the word, we receive an answer which is repeated with almost tedious monotony: the Spirit performs his work in the church *through the word*, as this word is found in the church's oral proclamation and in the sacraments. In the most profound sense "the word" means to Luther nothing else but Christ himself. Through the word, Christ himself, after his resurrection and ascension, is present among us, comes to us again in judgment and in grace, creates faith and thus builds his church on earth. Since the Spirit is the Spirit of Christ, the Spirit and his work are directly connected with "the external word" which is heard in the church. "In these matters, which concern the external, spoken Word, we must hold firmly to the conviction that God gives no one his Spirit or grace except through or with the external Word which comes before," Luther says in the Smalcald Articles. He continues in the same context: "Accordingly, we should and must constantly maintain that God will not deal with us except through his external Word and sacrament. Whatever is attributed to the Spirit apart from such Word and sacrament is of the devil."[1]

Since the Spirit is associated with the word, and the latter is found in Holy Scripture, the work of the Spirit becomes characteristically conceived of as connected with the word of Scripture itself. This word of which we speak here is not something that can be detached from these concrete texts, not "a freely soaring" word; but at the same

[1] The Smalcald Articles, in *The Book of Concord*, ed. Theodore G. Tappert (Philadelphia: Fortress Press, 1959), pp. 312-13.

time, the word is not simply identical with Scripture, if the reference is to the mere collection of writings. It is identical rather with the fact to which these writings as a whole bear witness, viz., Christ and the revelation given through him. This is the meaning of the commitment to the word of Scripture which characterizes the Reformation conception of the preaching of the church. As a word about Christ and the great work of God through him, this message even today is not only a gospel about Christ, but it is the life-giving word of Christ through which he comes to us now in the present just as in the days of the apostles. In order that we too may be drawn within this continuing act of salvation, "God has caused the Word to be published and proclaimed, in which he has given the Holy Spirit."[2] The word of Scripture is God's word and is united with the Spirit as it "goes forth and is proclaimed," and as it is directed toward people who hear and receive it.

It is characteristic that the word in this comprehensive meaning does not stand in opposition or in a complementary relationship to the sacraments. The word comes to us in various forms: in preaching, in private absolution, in baptism and the Lord's Supper. The common element in this unity is that the word is understood as active and not as "an instruction about something," or as "mere words." Just as baptism and the Lord's Supper are conceived of as an impartation of and a participation in Christ and in his righteousness and life, thus also the sermon is an impartation of

[2] The Large Catechism. *The Book of Concord*, p. 444.

Christ and his gifts. This is true also of the words of absolution directed to an individual person. In all this Christ himself is present with his Spirit, and therefore the word is a living and life-giving word, which in its encounter with men realizes and performs what it says. The word is an active word. It destroys and gives new birth, it creates faith and thus establishes the church of Christ on earth. "For through the Word and sacraments, as through instruments, the Holy Spirit is given, and the Holy Spirit produces faith, where and when it pleases God, in those who hear the Gospel."[3] The presence of the Spirit is not produced by or dependent upon our faith, it is rather his presence through the external word that creates faith.

Wherever the word functions in this manner, there is also the church, "the assembly of saints in which the Gospel is taught purely and the sacraments are administered rightly."[4] The Spirit performs his work in the church, which is "the mother that begets and bears every Christian"—and here Luther significantly completes his thought by adding "through the Word of God" and "the Holy Spirit reveals and preaches that Word."[5] "The church does not in herself have any life by which she can nurture her children, but life comes from the word because the Spirit performs his life-giving work only through the word. Through the word the Lord of the church continually comes to her, and he remains present and active through

[3] The Augsburg Confession, Article V. *Ibid.*, p. 31.
[4] The Augsburg Confession, Article VII. *Ibid.*, p. 32.
[5] The Large Catechism. *Ibid.*, p. 416.

his Spirit when this word is proclaimed publicly or privately or when it is offered in sacramental form. Where this happens there is also the church, precisely because the word is a creative and life-giving word and as such is never in vain. It is always the word of Christ, and therefore also "spirit and life" (John 6:63). Thus the word is the constitutive, creative and life-giving principle of the church.

The church's office of the ministry and the tasks of that ministry are incorporated in this conception of the word as actively associated with the Spirit and existing for the purpose of being offered and imparted to men in order to create faith. This office is not conceived of as simply a human ordinance. It is a divine institution which is based on the commission of Christ himself, "As the Father has sent me, even so I send you."[6] The indispensability of this office and its immense significance for the church appear most clearly when we consider the place which the article on "The Ministry of the Church" has been given in the Augsburg Confession. It follows immediately after the chief article on justification by faith. The article states: "In order that we may obtain this faith, the ministry of teaching the Gospel and administering the sacraments was instituted." Then follows the previously cited reference to the Spirit who is given "through the Word and the sacraments."[7]

[6] John 20:21. Cf. The Augsburg Confession, Article XXVIII. *Ibid.*, p. 81.
[7] The Augsburg Confession, Article V. *Ibid.*, p. 31. See above note 3, this chapter.

It is further stated in this same confession that through the gospel and the sacraments "it is not bodily things that are thus given, but rather such eternal things as eternal righteousness, the Holy Spirit, and eternal life. These things cannot come about except through the ministry of Word and sacraments." We can hardly imagine a stronger expression of the necessity of the ministry, but it is also significant that the text goes on to say: ". . . for Paul says, 'The gospel is the power of God for salvation to everyone who has faith,' and Ps. 119:50 states, 'Thy Word gives me life.' "[8]

When the Reformers speak of the ministry, they do not refer to something at the side of the gospel, but they are even in that connection speaking of this very same gospel which is of such a nature that it is "to be published and proclaimed." This is an idea that recurs again and again. When it is stated in the Apology of the Augsburg Confession that "the ministry of the Word has God's command and glorious promises," a reference is not made, as we perhaps might have expected, to some statement in the New Testament about the various ministries in the church, but to texts which speak of *the gospel* as "the power of God for salvation" (Rom. 1:16), and of *the Word* which goes forth from God's mouth, and does not return empty, but accomplishes his will (Isa. 55:11).[9]

The ministry is necessary because salvation and life are given through the word, the gospel, in its

[8] The Augsburg Confession, Article XXVIII. *Ibid.*, p. 82.
[9] Apology of the Augsburg Confession, Article XIII. *Ibid.*, p. 212.

various manifestations. The life-giving principle is
not the office per se, but the word this office has
to bear forth. For this reason the ministerial office
is often spoken of as *the ministry of the word*, and
this formula occurs again and again. This word,
in which Christ himself is present and active
through his Spirit, is nothing else than that found
in Scripture. As men are confronted with this word,
there is no difference in principle between the one
who has received the charge of the ministry and
his fellow Christians. They all together stand *under*
the word, and this means that they stand under
the same total judgment and the same total grace.
The difference lies in the fact that the incumbent
in the office has received a charge which the others
do not have. This subordination to the word finds
expression in the fact that the incumbent in the
office, in order to fulfill his task, has to go to the
word of Scripture and arduously use every means
to listen to what the texts have to say. It is not
a word over which he exercises authority, it is a
word which uses him in its service. It is not he
who "has to make the word alive," it is already
"the word of life." When we listen to the proclamation of the gospel, the sum of which is "to de-
nounce sin, to offer the forgiveness of sins and
righteousness for Christ's sake, to grant the Holy
Spirit and eternal life, and to lead us as regener-
ated men to do good,"[10] we listen to the Spirit and
therefore to the voice of Christ himself. The proclamation of the church is a living and life-giving

[10] Apology of the Augsburg Confession, Article XII. *Ibid.*,
pp. 185-86.

word, because and insofar as it extends to men
that word of life which is given in Holy Scripture.

The Spirit and the Ministry

If we approach Roman theology with our question, we receive an entirely different answer. Yet
here too it is apparent that the answer is provided
by the conception of the work of the Spirit in the
church, that Spirit who is "Lord and Giver of life."
Against the background of our previous presentation it is of special interest in this context to examine how Roman theology conceives of the relationship between the Spirit, Scripture and the
church.

It is not the case at all that Roman Catholic
theology should be unmindful of the connection
between the Spirit and the word of God given in
Scripture. In recent times few can match the en-
ergy with which Roman theologians have studied
the idea of the inspiration of Scripture and related
problems. But it is characteristic for this theology
that this affinity between the Spirit and the word
of Scripture is not, as with the Reformers, a matter
of the present. It is always regarded as belonging
to the past, and related exclusively to the origin
of the canonical writings. Scripture is indeed God's
word, but in the sense that in Scripture we find
words through which the Spirit of God *has spoken*
once upon a time, while the same Spirit *now* speaks
through the church and its ministry.

Here we must observe clearly that the relationship of the Spirit to the word of Scripture and to
the word of the church does not at all carry the

same importance. The Roman theologians differentiate clearly between the work of the Spirit that is designated by the term inspiration, which applies only to the canonical writings, and the assistance, *assistentia*, which the Spirit has given and continually gives to the teaching ministry of the church. In the former case it is a question of "revelation," but not in the latter. Revelation in the strict sense came to an end with the death of the last apostle, and the assistance which the Spirit thereupon gives to the church does not mean the communication of a new revelation. It means rather that the church now faithfully preserves and correctly interprets and expounds that content of the faith, *depositum fidei*, which was once for all given through revelation.

The decisive difference between the conceptions of the Reformation and of Roman theology in regard to the work of the Spirit in the church is not that only the former acknowledges a close connection between the Spirit and Scripture. The real difference appears only when we inquire about the proclamation of the church in the present, the active presence of the Spirit in the church now. While the Reformers combine the work of the Spirit with the message being proclaimed, i.e., with the word or gospel itself, we find in Roman Catholic theology an equally clear connection between the work of the Spirit and the institution which proclaims the gospel. The Holy Spirit is conceived of as *anima Ecclesiae*, "the soul" which makes the body of the church alive. This "body," this organism, animated and made alive by the Spirit,

is identical with the external, ecclesiastical institution. The Spirit is given to the church with the
intention that until the last day he shall constitute the inner and active nature and principle of
life in the church. The Spirit is one with the external, visible, juridical, hierarchical and organizational structure of the church. The church as such
is a visible manifestation of the Spirit himself.
This principle is stated by a Roman Catholic theologian in these words: the Spirit *verleiblicht sich in
der Kirche*, "the Spirit incarnates himself in the
church."[11]

The Spirit lives and works in the whole body of
the church, in all its members, but according to
a certain order. It is characteristic that this activity
is conceived of as taking place "in the inferior
members through the ministry of the higher members," *in inferioribus per superiorum ministerium*.
This phrase is from a statement by Pius XII in the
important encyclical of 1943 about the nature of
the church, *Mystici Corporis Christi*.[12] This statement means that the Spirit does not work directly
in the hearts of the faithful, but primarily through
a mediation by the hierarchical office of the church.
As soon as the work of the Spirit in the church is
spoken of, attention is immediately transferred to
the institution of the ministry itself. The life of
salvation, which comes from the Spirit, the in-
dwelling life principle of the church, flows as grace
through the bearers of the ministerial office to the

[11] T. Sartory, *Die ökumenische Bewegung und die Einheit
der Kirche* (Meitingen, 1955), p. 175.

[12] *Mystici Corporis Christi*, in Clarkson, *op. cit.*, p. 115.

faithful, sanctifying, strengthening and vivifying them.

It is from this context that we have to understand the development of the relationship between Scripture and the church which resulted in the ministry becoming the central and altogether decisive factor. The church through its teaching ministry has to preserve, defend and further expound that which once for all has been given. It is significant that this revelation, which has been lodged in Scripture and tradition, is regarded as something once handed over to the church, a *depositum*, which the church administers. This *depositum* is in itself without power and efficacy, a point of view that appears especially in statements about Holy Scripture. Scripture is in itself dead and powerless, and comes alive only as it is expounded by the teaching ministry of the church. We have noted above that the tradition of the church is defined as "a living tradition," and this is a direct consequence of the fact that it is sustained by the ministerial office in which the Spirit, "the Giver of life," is active. Life comes from the ministry of the church and from its word, not from the word of Scripture. The words of the Bible as written are dead and powerless, and they become alive only as they are used and activated in the living tradition of the church. The precedence of this tradition over Scripture lies precisely in that it is an expression of the work of the Spirit *now*, that Spirit who does not dwell in dead documents but in the living voice of the ministry. Apart from the teaching ministry of the church the Bible is a dead letter and a sealed book.

In this context Roman Catholics do not speak of the word of Scripture but of the words of the ministry as "living words," and especially about the office itself as "a living teaching ministry," *vivum magisterium*. This designation appears again and again both in papal encyclicals and in dogmatic presentations. When it is said that the Spirit is "incarnate" in the church, we must understand this primarily as a statement about the ministry. Thus it is possible also to speak of the office as "an objectification of the Holy Spirit."[13] The designation "living" is applied to the ministerial office precisely because the Spirit now in the church does not speak through the words of Scripture, which in themselves are dead and spiritless, but through the living voice of the ministry. Here, in contrast to Luther, there is no notion that the proclamation of the church is alive because it reproduces the message that is found in Scripture; rather, its living and life-giving character follows from the fact that it is *not* tied to "the dead letter" of Scripture.

When Roman theologians on this point compare their own position to that of the Reformers, they contrast their "personal principle" (the living ministry) to what they call the Reformers' "factual principle" [*Sach Prinzip*] (Scripture). The German dogmatist M. Schmaus expresses this idea very clearly when he says that in order to listen to the apostolic voice we do not have to turn to

[13] T. Sartory, *op. cit.*, p. 174. *Der sich im Amt objektivierende Heilige Geist.*

"literature," but to "living bearers of authority." Faith comes from preaching, and the reference therefore is not to "the dead letter" but to the living proclamation.[14]

It is evident, however, that here that which is characteristic of Luther has not yet been discovered. He too can speak of "the dead letter" of Scripture, but it is significant that the contrast is not in this case between "dead Scripture" and "spiritually sustained *oral* tradition." The contrast is rather between the content of Scripture understood as "law" and the content of Scripture understood as "gospel." Moreover, this gospel is not primarily a "book," but a word that is proclaimed and offered to men who hear and receive it. In this context too faith is directed away from "the dead letter" to the living proclamation, although this involves not a reference to the *ministry of the church*, but to the *gospel*. In one sense we could say that this involves a "material principle," because everything depends on the proclamation of that "fact" which Scripture contains; but at the same time it is a question of "a personal principle," because this "fact" is, in the last analysis, nothing else than Christ himself who comes to us in the preaching of the word.

From the point of view of the association between the Spirit and the ministry which characterizes Roman Catholic theology, we can understand more clearly an issue previously discussed, the development of dogma in the church. Since the Spirit himself is the soul and life principle in

[14] M. Schmaus, *op. cit.*, III: 1, pp. 186, 189 f., 765.

the living organism of the church—an organism which has developed from the modest beginning of the ancient church until today—it is accordingly its work that has enabled the church to grow in insight into the content of that faith which was given once for all in the revelation and which continues to be administered by the church. The church in Scripture and in the oldest tradition indeed possessed the revelation and thereby also the saving truth, but it had not attained to the perfect and comprehensive insight into that truth which the church of today has reached by the guidance of the Spirit, and which is expressed especially in the Marian dogmas.

Unity with the primitive church is not guaranteed by the fact that the message of the church now conforms to what the apostles once proclaimed. As related to the notion of an organism this demand would appear unreasonable. This unity is guaranteed rather by the fact that *the one and the same Spirit*, who once spoke through the apostles, now speaks through their successors in the teaching office of the church. The certainty that the church thereby reproduces what the Spirit wants to say is not based on any demonstrable conformity between Scripture and what is spoken, it is derived rather from the church itself. The Spirit does not *now* speak through the words of Scripture, but through the church and her words. A contradiction between the living tradition of the church and Scripture is in principle excluded, since the Spirit cannot contradict himself.

It is furthermore impossible to find any departure from the truth in the church's interpretation of the content of revelation as set forth by the teaching ministry, since, inasmuch as the Spirit dwells in the church, all the sources out of which errors could arise are closed. And "the most important of these sources [of errors] is an unyielding insistence on the dead letter of the Bible."[15] To go to Scripture without the complementary interpretation which the living tradition of the church provides does not mean that one goes to the source of truth, but rather that one enters upon a road that leads away from truth and the Spirit of truth. From this point of view it becomes abundantly clear why the teaching ministry of the church is continually designated as the immediate and primary rule of faith.

The association between the Spirit and the living voice of the church in the present, which we continually encounter, helps to clarify also the appearance of the dogma of the infallibility of the Pope. The teaching ministry of the church is concentrated in the Pope, and his infallibility in questions of doctrine is based ultimately on that special *assistentia* with which the Spirit supports him as the vicar of Christ on earth. This is not a new idea. When Boniface VIII in his well-known bull of 1302 *Unam Sanctam*, declared that it was necessary for every man's salvation to be subject to the Pope, he motivated this claim by an exposition of I Corinthians 2:15. He interprets this passage about

---

[15] *Die wichtigste dieser Quellen ist das Sichversteifen auf den toten Buchstaben der Bibel.* K. Algermissen, *Konfessionskunde* (7th ed.; Celle, 1957), p. 156.

"the spiritual man" who "judges all things" but
is himself to be "judged by no one" as a reference
to Peter, and therefore also to all his successors in
the papal chair. The Pope is "the spiritual man"
through whom the Spirit now speaks and therefore
a modern Roman theologian can identify "the age
of the Spirit" with "the age of the primacy of the
Pope."[16] Where the Pope is, there is Christ; where
Christ is, there is also his Spirit; and where the
Spirit is, there is the church.

This does not mean, however, that the ordinary
priest, or even the Pope himself, can simply and
arbitrarily establish his own points of view as
authoritative and divine words. Just as in the
evangelical conception of the ministry it is characteristic that the minister must listen to the word
of Scripture, so also Roman theology maintains
firmly that the ministry itself must listen and learn
in order to be able to proclaim the message it has
to bear forth. Even here the incumbent in the
ministerial office has the inescapable task of listening, but in the very center of this common attitude
the difference becomes unmistakably clear. He
does not primarily have to listen to the word given
in Scripture, but to the church and to what the
Spirit says through the living tradition of the
church. Only afterward he can go to the Bible. In
order to fulfill its task the teaching ministry of
today must listen to and discern what the same
teaching ministry has said during earlier generations.[17] But this means that in the last analysis the

[16] Ch. Journet, *L'Eglise du Verbe Incarne* I (2nd ed.; Paris,
1955), p. 517.
[17] Ch. Journet, *op. cit.*, II (1951), p. 638.

teaching office has to listen to itself and its own voice. It is not the word, but the ministerial office of the church which is the creative, life-giving and constitutive principle of the church. The Spirit works through this office, and *therefore* the proclamation of the church is a living and life-giving word. When one listens to the ministerial office, one hears the voice of the Spirit.

The Spirit as Lord

In the center of the common confession of the Spirit as "Lord and Giver of life" we find, therefore, a decisive line of division between the evangelical and the Roman views. That with which the Spirit is associated becomes immediately the authoritative and life-giving principle.[18] If we assume that the Spirit works through the word encountered in Scripture, it is this word which bestows salvation and life, and which also appears as lord and authority over the church's ministry. The authority of the ministry is nothing else than the authority of the word, "the authority of the ministry depends on the Word of God."[19] The authority of the word of the ministry does not reside in the office as such. It is nothing else than the authority of the word itself, its active power to accuse and judge, but also to restore, renew and set free from sin. He who has received the commission of the ministry does not thereby become superior to or

[18] Cf. George S. Hendry, *The Holy Spirit in Christian Theology* (Philadelphia: Westminster, 1957), pp. 53 ff.
[19] Treatise on the Power and Primacy of the Pope. *The Book of Concord, op. cit.,* p. 321.

master over the word; he himself, just as others, is subject to the word which judges and restores everyone including him.

If, on the contrary, we assume that the Spirit works primarily through the ministry, we then conceive of the office as the power-filled authority in the church, that life-giving spring out of which salvation flows. Then one no longer asks "what the *word* says," but "what the *church* is saying," because the decisive point is not *what* is said, but *who* says it. The most important matter for the church will then be not the question about the purity of the gospel, but the question about the validity of the ministry. The authority to which one must listen is not the word found in Scripture, but the infallible *interpretation* of the word of Scripture by the ministry which is superior to the word itself. Not the word, but the office, is here lord. Even though both sides diligently speak of the proclamation of the church as *viva vox*, it soon becomes apparent that the reference is to two different things. Behind the common terminology we discern the decisive antithesis between *viva vox evangelii*, the living voice of the gospel, and *viva vox magisterii*, the living voice of the teaching ministry.

Roman Catholics speak frequently of the firm and confident authority which they possess in the infallible word of the teaching office of the church. They frequently compare this single authority with the numerous and sometimes contradictory interpretations found in evangelical theology. But they do not see that in the midst of this chorus of many

voices there is also the deepest unity, because all
the different interpreters listen to the word of
Scripture. The very dissension bears witness to
the fact that this word itself is conceived of as
authority and lord. This dignity must not be
attributed to the individual interpretation. When
that happens, the scriptural principle of the Reformation is abandoned, because this means that
one has ceased to listen to him who through the
word comes to his church, and instead is self-com-
placently listening to one's own interpretation.
"Pure doctrine" is not something that can be held
as a secure possession, it must be reclaimed in
every new age and in every new situation by a
collective hearing of the word and a struggle
against false doctrine as it continually arises.

When one abandons this open and listening
attitude toward the word and toward others, it is
a sign that one expects salvation and life to come
from one's own thoughts and opinions rather than
from Christ alone who in his word comes to us
with judgment and restoration. It is also a sign
that one is going away from the teaching about
the Spirit and the word which characterized the
Reformation, and which is found in the confessional writings of the Reformation churches.

The Spirit is the Spirit of Jesus Christ. Where
he is active, the confession of Christ as Lord comes
forth (I Cor. 12:3). The crucified, risen and as-
cended Lord of the church is now himself present
among his own in his Spirit. "The Lord is the
Spirit" (II Cor. 3:17). Wherever he is present,
something happens; "we all . . . are being changed

into his likeness" (II Cor. 3:18), because the presence of the Spirit is nothing else than God's own
personal, creative, active and life-giving presence,
through which men are incorporated into Christ
in his death and resurrection in order to become
like him.

The life-giving work of the Spirit always takes
place in a struggle with "the flesh" in all its various manifestations. It was thus even in the circle
of the first apostles, who constituted the church at
its beginning. There was Thomas the doubter,
Judas the betrayer, and Peter who denied. Paul
at one time in Antioch even had to remonstrate
against Peter. Here "the truth of the gospel" (Gal.
2:14) stood forth as the authority even over the
apostles, "the pillars" in the church (Gal. 2:9).
Already at this point it is the gospel, not the ministry as such, which is the authority and lord. But
this is the same as saying that the Spirit is Lord,
for to listen to the gospel is to listen to the voice of
the Spirit. The Spirit is sent *to* the church in order
that the word of Christ may be proclaimed, "he
will take what is mine and declare it to you"
(John 16:14). The letters in Revelation 2-3 are the
word of the *Lord* to Christian churches, and here
it behooves us to hear "what the *Spirit* says *to* the
churches" (Rev. 2:29; 3:22).

Since the Spirit is God's own powerful presence,
it is impossible to identify him with an immanent
principle of life in the church, or with some powers
active in the church. He works *in* the church, but
as God he also confronts the church as a person
over against whom the church as a whole stands

in a relationship of obedience, and from whom she receives her life. This is what Luther and the confessions strive to express when they uncompromisingly insist that the Spirit works only through "the external word." This word is to be proclaimed *by* the church, but it does not on this account cease to be a word *to* the church itself. When the Spirit is separated from this word and instead becomes identified with an inner illumination alongside the testimony of Scripture to Christ, then in the last analysis it is not the voice of the Spirit that we hear, but our own voice and our own opinions. This is true whether this illumination is thought of as being given to all Christians, as the "radical Reformers" in the time of Luther and later taught, or only to the incumbents in the office of the ministry, as in Roman Catholic teaching. Then we expect truth and life to come from ourselves, not "from the outside," and "the external word" in Scripture is conceived of primarily as a means to confirm and uphold the opinions at which we have already arrived.

This means that in spite of all claims to a firm and confident authority residing in the infallible teaching office, there is in reality no authority at all, because an authority can only be something by which we are confronted. If we assume that there is a real confrontation between the Spirit and the church, then "infallibility" becomes an impossible attitude, because to stand before him who is "Lord" must always mean that we stand in a relationship of obedience and are willing to be corrected. In the presence of God and his word no one can stand as "infallible." When the church withdraws from that word, which even to her is a word of judgment and restoration, and instead listens to her own voice, she also withdraws from life, because it is specifically as a word of judgment on all our works and opinions that the word of Christ is a life-giving word. The Spirit is not an immanent quality that guarantees our excellencies, he is God himself who comes to us to recreate and transform, "this comes from the Lord who is the Spirit" (II Cor. 3:18). If the gospel is conceived of simply as a word coming from the church itself and its ministry, we can no longer perceive of Christ as coming *to* his church and encountering her in judgment and grace. In that case the ministry removes itself from judgment in order that by *itself* it may take over Christ's place as the source of grace for the other members of the church, and become judge and lord over them. But he who in everything is his own master and only listens to himself, is in reality without a Lord, and consequently abandoned to a really serious insecurity.

IV

CHRIST AND THE MINISTRY OF THE CHURCH

Our previous discussion has been concerned with an analysis of Roman and evangelical statements which initially appear very similar, but in point after point we have found an important divergence in meaning. This decisive difference between Roman and evangelical conceptions might perhaps be summarized in the proposition that in the Roman Catholic position everything revolves around the *ministry* of the church, while in the evangelical conception the central element is the *gospel* which is derived from Scripture and is now active in the church. But this does not mean, as is also evident from our previous discussion, that from the evangelical point of view the ministry of the church is without significance. On the contrary, precisely for the sake of the gospel the ministry is a necessary factor in the life of the church. Furthermore, since the question of the ministry occupies a central place in our present ecumenical and theological discussions, it might be quite proper finally to subject the conception of the ministry to a more precise and closer examination.

In making this examination we may proceed from what has been said in the previous chapter about the proclamation of the church. Even as both parties can speak of this proclamation as "a living word," so we also find that both sides emphasize strongly the *authoritative* character of this word. In this connection they often quote the words of Jesus to his disciples in Luke 10:16: "He who hears you hears me." This is the case, for example, in the encyclical of 1950 *Humani generis* by Pius XII, where the Pope strongly affirms that this word of Christ has reference to what is said in the church through the ministry, and that consequently this ministry speaks with the authority of Christ himself. The same manner of expression is also to be found in the Lutheran confessional books. Thus the Apology of the Augsburg Confession in speaking of "the power of the keys" exercised by the ministry of the church says: "Because God truly quickens through the Word, the keys truly forgive sin before him, according to the statement (Luke 10:16), 'He who hears you hears me.' Therefore we must believe the voice of the one absolving no less than we would believe a voice coming from heaven."[1] On both sides the ministry is conceived of as instituted by God and as such it performs a necessary function, necessary

[1] Apology of the Augsburg Confession, Article XII. *The Book of Concord, op. cit.*, p. 187.

in order that the voice of Christ shall be heard in the church.

But even here the paths diverge as soon as we ask for the reason why the words and the acts of the ministry are spoken of on both sides as Christ's own word and Christ's own work.

The Ministry as a Representation of Christ

To the above question Roman Catholic theology answers by speaking of an identity between Christ's own functions in his ministry and the objectives which are now constitutive for the ministry of the church. Thus in his encyclical on the liturgy of the church *Mediator Dei* (1947), Pope Pius XII stated that Christ, the incarnate word, and the church have the same task and the same ministry. In this case Roman theology may, following an old tradition, speak of Christ as having a twofold office as king and priest; or, using a threefold conception taken over from Protestant theological tradition and now dominant in Roman theology, it may speak of Christ's threefold office as prophet, king, and priest. Whichever pattern is used, these statements about Christ and his work are immediately also conceived of as statements about the ministry of the church and its functions. The latter are interpreted as an extension and a continuation of Christ's own work. This conception is centralized in the idea of the ministry of the church as *"a representation of Christ."* In the ministry of the church Christ is present "anew," and therefore the church through its ministry is in a way the con-

tinuation of the living Christ here on earth, a
re-praesentatio of the Incarnate.

The prophetic office of Christ continues in the
function of the church's office as a teaching ministry; Christ's kingly office continues in the church's
pastoral ministry with its power to rule; and
Christ's (high) priestly office has its continuation
in the priestly function of the church's ministry.
All these functions together constitute the ministry
of the church in its fullness, and in them Christ
himself, his words and his works, is represented in
the church in every age.

When it is said that the *teaching ministry* of
the church constitutes a continuation of the prophetic office of Christ, it does not mean that the
preaching of the church is a continuation of the
revelation given through Christ. This revelation,
which belongs to the time of the founding of the
church, has a unique character and cannot be continued in succeeding generations. But precisely
this which has once for all been given now appears
in the proclamation of the church; it is administered by the church, interpreted and proclaimed
continually to new generations. When one listens,
therefore, to the teaching ministry of the church,
one hears Christ's own voice, because the ministry
actualizes that which was once given in the revelation and brings it anew into the present. Just as
Christ through his Spirit was once present and
active through the apostles, so he is now present
and active through that ministry which represents
him in the church of today. The words of the
church, therefore, are at the same time Christ's

own words, and the preaching of the church is Christ's witness to himself, *ein Selbstzeugnis Christi*.[2]

It then becomes quite natural that this idea of a representation of Christ, which is fundamental for the conception of the ministry, appears also as a justification for the dogma of the infallibility of the Pope. Since the office of the Pope constitutes a concentration of the teaching ministry of the church, we also find in this office a concentration of the ministry's representation of Christ. In the Pope, who is "as it were Christ made visible in the church as a whole,"[3] the believer now meets Christ himself in a visible form, and therefore it is just as impossible to assume that the Pope could err in matters of doctrine as to think that Christ could do so. The voice of the Pope is the voice of Christ here and now. On the basis of this characteristically Roman conception of the ministry as a representation of Christ, any appeal to an authority superior to the teaching ministry is an impossibility, because in the last analysis it would imply that one placed something else above the voice of Christ himself.

Even the governing authority of Christ, which constitutes his kingly office, has since his departure been transmitted to the apostles and their successors. This applies primarily to the bishops who are in communion with the Pope as the successor of Peter and consequently possess the apostolic succession. They now together with the Pope oc-

[2] M. Schmaus, *op. cit.*, III: 1, p. 798.
[3] M. Schmaus, *op. cit.*, I, p. 35.

cupy *the pastoral office* in the church. Just as Christ was "lawgiver" (*legislator*, a designation which the Council of Trent emphasized in contrast to the Reformers) in that he came with the "new law" of the gospel, thus also the pastoral office, as it represents him, appears as a lawgiving and governing power in the church. It is not a question here of a "new" governing power by the side of Christ, just as in reference to the teaching office there was no suggestion of a "new" revelation. It is rather Christ's own authority during his life on earth which is now exercised by the pastoral office of the church, and included in this authority is also *inter alia* the exercise of the power of the keys, the power to bind in sin and to loose from sin.

The very division of the church's limbs into primary and secondary as demanded by the juridical character of the church, is in Roman theology referred back to the institution of Christ himself and constitutes, therefore, something essential for the church. Thus by calling the disciples as special incumbents of office, Christ has established the differentiation between priests and laymen which is fundamental for the nature of the church. Furthermore, by giving to Peter (and thereby also to his successors) an authority over the other apostles, he has created a hierarchical division into levels of authority even within the incumbents in the ministerial office.

The power of the kingly office is concentrated in the office of the Pope, just as is the authority for teaching, which is often reckoned as a subdivision of the former. The Pope, as the possessor of the highest legislative and governing power within the church, is the vicar of Christ and the visible head of the church. This does not mean, however, that it is now the Pope who "instead of Christ" governs the church on earth, or that the body of the church is a monstrosity with two heads. Even in his pastoral function the Pope is a representative of Christ in the sense that his authority to govern is an expression of Christ's own rule. Christ himself acts in and through the Pope, and thus continues, even though invisible, to rule his church.

That the Pope is the vicar of Christ means, therefore, practically the opposite to the notion that Christ now has withdrawn and transferred the church to someone else. It means rather that Christ now and until his return appears in visible and audible form in the acts and works of the Pope, *im Tun des Papstes wird Christus selbst hör- und sichtbar*.[4] In the mystical body of the church Christ and his vicar on earth are not two but one and the same head, as Pius XII in a frequently-used formula points out in his encyclical *Mystici Corporis Christi* (1943).[5] But this means, as Pius XII emphasizes in this context, that it is not possible for anyone to abide in Christ without at the same time faithfully clinging to his representative on earth. Since the Pope is the vicar of Christ, obedience to him is equivalent to obedience to Christ himself.

[4] M. Schmaus, *op. cit.*, III: 1, p. 488.
[5] *Mystici Corporis Christi*, in Clarkson, *op. cit.*, p. 111.

While the powers of both the teaching and the pastoral offices appear in a hierarchically-graduated scale with a concentration in the primacy of the Pope, and while their exercise is restricted to specific persons and areas, the *priestly* office in the proper sense constitutes a function which everyone who has been separated from the laity by the sacrament of ordination performs in the whole church without restrictions. This priestly function is a continuation or an extension of the high-priestly office of Christ, and consequently even in this case the bearer of the office is a representative of Christ.

The duties of the priestly office are performed especially in the sacrifice of the Mass for the living and the dead, and further in the administration of the sacraments and in the sacrifice of prayer and praise in the service of the canonical hours. Christ himself entrusted his priestly office to the apostles at their last common meal with the words: "Do this in remembrance of me." The Council of Trent established this interpretation as the only one permissible, and since that time this idea recurs continually in Roman Catholic theology. The words of Jesus to the apostles meant that they were appointed as the sacrificial priests of the new covenant, and this authority has since then been transmitted to new generations of incumbents in the office through the sacrament of ordination.

The most important task of the priest is the sacrifice of the Mass. In Protestant presentations we frequently meet the idea, which seems to survive tenaciously, that the Roman church speaks of a "repetition" of the sacrifice which Christ once for all completed on the cross. This is a rather misleading conception. Roman theology, too, knows and emphatically affirms the unique and absolute character of the sacrifice on Golgotha. Just as Roman theology does not speak about any "new" revelation or a "new" kingly office by the side of Christ as king, so neither is there a question here about a "new" sacrifice. Instead *the identity* between the sacrifice of Christ and the sacrifice of the Mass is continually emphasized. It is the sacrifice of Christ, and nothing else, that the priest through his words and actions "makes present" on the altar. Because it is a matter of *re-praesentatio*, a *re*presentation of Christ's unique and perfectly valid sacrifice, what happens can also be defined as a renewal, a *renovatio*, of the sacrifice on the cross, because it is precisely this sacrifice which is present "anew" through the action of the priest. The difference between the two sacrifices is found in the manner in which the sacrifice is offered. The bloody sacrifice on Golgotha is present in the Mass in an "unbloody" manner.

This identity between the sacrifice on Golgotha and the sacrifice of the Mass is generally stated in such a way that in each case we have the *same* sacrificial gift and the *same* officiating priest, thus following a formula established by the Council of Trent. It is the same sacrificial gift, *hostia*, because it is Christ himself who at the climax of the Mass, the miracle of transubstantiation, is present in the transformed elements.

But the presence of the sacrificial gift does not

constitute the sacrifice, because a "sacrifice" is not
only a sacrificial gift, but primarily an action of
which the gift is the object. It is this action performed by the priest which is the decisive factor
in the sacrifice, but when the priest performs this
action, he does not act on his own authority, but
as a representative of Christ. In the Mass he plays
"the part of Christ," an expression that is frequently used, because in the moment of his ordination he has received "the power to perform in
the church the sacrifice for the living and the
dead," and consequently he acts "in the person and
power of Christ," *in persona et virtute Christi*. In
order that there might be a *re-praesentatio* of the
sacrifice of Christ in the Mass, it is necessary first
of all that there be a *re-praesentatio* of Christ
himself in the holder of the office. This ability of
the priest to represent Christ, which he has received
through his ordination, is the necessary condition
for the presence of Christ in the elements. The
presence of Christ in the church is here primarily
a presence in and through the ministry of the
church.

The idea of the sacrifice of the Mass as a
re-praesentatio of the sacrifice of Christ appears,
therefore, as a special instance of the general conception of representation which determines the
view of all the functions of the ecclesiastical office.
Everywhere we are dealing with something which
Christ once entrusted to the church and which now
is made present and active "anew" through the
bearer of the office who represents Christ himself.
Thus the church administers the revealed content

of the faith, *depositum fidei*, which only through the exposition by the ministry becomes a life-giving word. The same is true about the power of the keys, which has not been given to the whole church, as the Reformers held, but only to the ministry. On an analogy with these functions Roman Catholics speak also of the sacrifice of Christ as something entrusted to the church, which becomes a redemptive action for men of today only when it is actualized and presented anew by the priest who represents Christ.

Since everything revolves around the ministerial office, the acts of consecration through which the functions of the ministry of Christ are transmitted to new bearers of the office receive a tremendously central and decisive significance for salvation. Thus in the encyclical *Mediator Dei* (1947), Pius XII pointed out that the sacrament of ordination establishes within the church a line of demarcation of the same decisive character as that which through baptism is established between Christians and non-Christians.[6] Actually even baptism places an indelible stamp upon the Christian by conforming him to Christ, and the essential nature of the ordination is likewise that it bestows upon the priest an indelible likeness to Christ. Here, however, we are not dealing with an intensified likeness to Christ in comparison with that given in baptism, but rather it is a likeness of an entirely different nature, viz., the ability to represent Christ in the church, or to "play the role of Christ." He who is ordained to the priesthood is taken out of the congregation

[6] *Mediator Dei*, in Denzinger, *op. cit.*, pp. 627-28.

and placed over against it as an image of Christ
himself.

What this conception means more specifically
can be seen most clearly if we consider what
Roman theology frequently does in its interpretation of the New Testament statements about the
church as the bride of Christ, the body of Christ
and the new people of God. On the basis of the
representation idea these statements are interpreted
as statements about the relationship between the
ministry of the church and the laymen. Thus it
is said that, when the church is spoken of as the
bride of Christ, this does not refer to the church as
a whole, but only to the lay people. The ordained
bearers of the office, on the other hand, represent
the bridegroom, Christ, over against the laymen.
Correspondingly the image of the church as the
body of Christ is interpreted along the same line.
Here the bearers of the office constitute the visible
manifestation of the head of the church over
against the rest of the members. The same interpretation is applied to the statement of the church
as the people of God: the bearer of the office "dis-
plays God whose people is the church"[7]—in him
"the people" meet God himself in visible form.
Translated into the concrete situation of the congregation this means that the laity encounter and
obtain salvation only by way of contact with the
bearer of the office, because in him they come in
contact with and encounter the Savior himself.

[7] The bearer of the office *stellt den Gott dar, dessen Volk
die Kirche ist.* Cf. O. Semmelroth, *Das Geistliche Amt*
(Frankfurt, 1958), pp. 27, 41.

The bearer of the office does not only represent Christ over against the congregation, but he also in his person represents the congregation, the laity, "the people," before God. This representative function, however, is not primary, but is regarded as a consequence of the fact that the priest through his ordination has become a representative of Christ. As such he continues and completes the office of Christ as mediator, and is therefore, as Christ himself, not only God's representative toward men, but also their representative toward God. When in the Mass the priest on behalf of the whole congregation brings the sacrifice of Christ to God as an expiatory offering, his action is a valid sacrifice not because he represents the congregation, but because he represents Christ. The believers' offering of themselves to God becomes valid and acceptable only by being included in the sacrificial action of the priest who represents Christ; only his action possesses such power. Since the priest's sacrifice includes the others already, because through his ordination he has become a representative of Christ, his sacrifice does not in any sense receive its power and validity from the congregation. Consequently, this sacrifice can just as well be offered without the presence of a congregation. This private Mass without a congregation is, therefore, consistent with the conception of the priest as a representative of Christ. The communion of the faithful is indeed a desirable but not a necessary element in the Mass, since its essential nature is a sacrificial action which can be performed only by the priest ordained for this purpose.

When with the lines of thought developed under

the influence of evangelical theology we encounter the statements about the ministers of the church as "substitutes," "representatives," or "vicars," we are prone to interpret them to mean that Christ after his life on earth has passively withdrawn and turned over his church to others, who now "in his stead" continue his work. One would now therefore no longer have to deal with Christ himself in any real sense, but with his representatives. But this is a gross misinterpretation. It would be more true to say that the idea of representation is intended precisely to express Christ's actual and effective presence in the church of today. Christ constitutes not only the first link in the unbroken chain of bearers of the office through the ages, he is rather the one who actually in them is present and active in every generation. The ministry of the church is the form in which the invisible Christ after his ascension is now tangibly present, speaking and acting in his church. For this reason the voice of the Pope is the voice of Christ, and the priest's sacrificial act is a visible manifestation of Christ's own sacrifice. In summarizing one could say that the ministry of the church as representative of Christ constitutes a visualization of the invisibly present Christ.

Christology and the Roman Conception of the Ministry

The idea of representation involves a peculiar combination of Christology and the conception of the ministry. When Roman theologians speak of Christ and his work, their statements apply also to the ministry and its function because the ministry now plays the part of Christ. This means that if we are to understand the factors which produce such a conception of the ministry, we must consider the Roman Catholic Christology. In this connection it is obvious that we can consider only a few features which are decisive in reference to the conception of the ministry.

A common objection by Roman Catholic theology to the evangelical point of view is that evangelical theology fails to take the incarnation, i.e., God becoming man in Christ, seriously. This is made more concrete in the assertion that ever since Luther evangelical thought has undervalued the humanity of Christ, his "human nature." In direct contrast, his human nature has a central position in Roman theology, in the sense that it is this human nature of Christ, united with the divine, which "in a perfect way causes and mediates salvation."[8] Because of its union with the divine word his humanity is "full of grace and truth." In it the divine grace is apprehensibly and tangibly present in the world, and salvation is mediated through "contact" with this human nature of Christ. (The word "contact" occurs frequently in this connection.) Since this means of salvation was taken away from the earth by the ascension, the problem arises how one shall now come into contact with that divine grace on which salvation depends. It is at this point that the ministry of the church comes into the picture. Christ transferred his own functions to it and its bearers, and they constitute there-

[8] C. Lialine, in *En bok om kyrkans ämbete* (Stockholm, 1951), p. 126.

fore "a second human nature of Christ," which just
like Christ's own humanity is "an effective means
of salvation" in the church, even though it is not
connected with the divine in exactly the same
way.[9] In this way "the contact" which is necessary
for and provides salvation is secured and made
possible in a continuous manner. The church is
created out of the saving and life-giving contact
with that ministry which now plays the same role
in the church as Christ's humanity did before his
ascension. In the words and acts of the holders of
the office, in the word and sacraments of the
church, one now encounters and partakes of that
grace and truth which came into the world through
the incarnation.

Consequently it also becomes clear why questions
about the valid ministry, valid succession and valid
ordination come to be of such crucial importance
in this connection. They are questions concerning
the primary means of salvation in the church,
questions on which her whole life depends. The
ministry constitutes the fundamental element in
the church, because to ask about the valid ministry
is the same as asking about salvation itself. From
this point of view it also becomes evident why the
separation between the consecrated ministry and
the laity in the church is regarded as something
constitutive for the nature of the church and too
precious to be lost. It is a cleavage necessary for
salvation itself, because without the bearers of the
office, who have been set apart from the multitude
of the baptized in order to represent Christ him-

[9] *Ibid.*, pp. 126 ff.

self, and therefore to mediate grace, redemptive contact with Christ would no longer be possible.

In this context we should also note the decisive importance attributed to the fact that the redemptive work of Christ is precisely a *human* activity. As a Roman theologian explains this conception, in what is actually a direct polemic against Luther, it is not here a question of "God in Christ," but of Christ's holy humanity, which "in itself and as human, albeit on the basis of its union with the divine, is holy and sanctifying."[10] The human nature of Christ is united with God as that "organ" or "instrument" through which the redemptive work is accomplished. But this instrument is not a dead and volitionless tool which mechanically follows the divine intention, but being human it maintains its own free activity. Christ as human chooses voluntarily to participate in the work of redemption, and this participation takes place precisely as a real human activity, as it were, on the side of or parallel with the divine. This conception appears not least in the interpretation of the sacrifice of Christ on the cross as a human achievement rendered to God. This achievement derives its eternal value from the intimate union of the human nature with God, and is therefore conditioned upon and an expression of the divine grace. But it is at the same time altogether a work of Christ as man, and is thereby an expression of that free and independent activity which according to

[10] Y. M. J. Congar, *Le Christ, Marie et l'Eglise* (Paris, 1952), p. 66 English trans., by Henry St. John, *Christ, Our Lady and the Church* (Westminster, Md.: Newman Press, 1957).

the Roman Catholic conception characterizes man
in his relationship to God. This voluntary cooperation on the part of the human element is absolutely
necessary if salvation is to become effective.

We encounter, therefore, in the christological
doctrine itself the idea of a *cooperation* between
the divine and the human which generally characterizes the Roman Catholic conception of the
relationship to God. Salvation is attained by a
cooperation between grace and the free will of
man, his *liberum arbitrium*, a term in common use
since the days of scholasticism. In one sense salvation is God's work and takes place through "grace
alone," because without this grace no salvation is
possible. But in another sense it is at the same time
the work of man, because final salvation is obtained
through the meritorious works which man accomplishes with the help of grace. This conception of
salvation as something which ultimately comes
through a cooperation between the divine and the
human is the impelling motif behind the interpretation of the meaning of the ministry which we
have found in our previous discussion. The humanity of Christ is conceived of in union with the
divine as a freely acting medium in its own right,
and through it salvation is effected. This partic-
ular view of the relationship between the human
and the divine in Christ demands that the notion
of human cooperation be continued in respect to
the ministry, because salvation is brought about
through the cooperation of two elements and if
one of them is lacking, salvation itself in the last
analysis ceases to exist. This is perfectly natural,

since salvation is always obtained, now as during the life of Jesus on earth, through a cooperation between the divine and the human. Since the humanity of Christ is now absent from the world, its work must be continued by others who stand in its stead and assume its role. This is the reason why the ministry comes to be regarded as "a second human nature of Christ." It is significant that according to Roman Catholic Christology Christ performs his threefold ministry as prophet, king and priest precisely *as man;* and, therefore, these functions of the ministry of Christ can also be continued *by men* who constitute "an effective means of salvation in the church," since they in this way "play the role of Christ." But this does *not* mean that the incumbents in the ministry by this activity "repeat" or do the work of Christ "over again." This would simply be an impossibility, since, as the work of *Christ,* it has a unique character and eternal validity, because it has been performed by a human nature in union with the divine itself. The work of the ministerial office is not a new work of salvation by the side of that of Christ, but it means rather that through the priest's action the redemptive act of *Christ* becomes present and effective anew in the church. The priest does not act on his own authority, but on the authority of Christ. He does not represent himself, but Christ. Ordination to the ministry does not mean a new incarnation, but extends and brings into the present that which through the incarnation of Christ came into the world. This is what is meant by the frequent saying that the church is "an extension of the incarnation," or "Christ as continually living in the world." That grace, which once was mediated through direct contact with the Incarnate, is now mediated only through contact with the church and its ministry.

The conception of a human cooperation in the work of redemption, which we have analyzed above, and which is determinative for the concept of representation, also characterizes another circle of ideas typical in modern Roman Catholic theology, viz., *Mariology*. There is, consequently, a remarkable parallel between the conception of the ministry and the interpretation of the role of Mary in the work of redemption. Thus it is said that it is through Mary that salvation becomes available to men. She is the mediatrix between men and Christ. Just as no one comes to the Father but through the Son, so no one comes to the Son but through Mary, as Leo XIII states in his encyclical of 1891 *Octobri mense*.[11] Furthermore, in theological presentations we constantly encounter Mary as *dispensatrix* or *mediatrix omnium gratiarum*. All grace comes to men through her intercession and mediation. Like the church Mary is designated as the mother of all the faithful, and through her both Christ and the Spirit are bestowed. In the moment of the Annunciation the whole work of redemption depends on her "yes" to the angel, she brings Christ by birth into the world, and through her cooperation grace and truth come to men. In his encyclical on the church (1943), Pius XII says that it was Mary who through her prayers brought

[11] *Octobri mense,* in Denzinger, *op. cit.,* p. 488.

it about that the Spirit was sent to the apostles on Pentecost. In the same context we are told how Mary brought her Son on Golgotha as a sacrifice to the eternal Father—a direct parallel to the function of the priest in the sacrifice of the Mass. All these ideas may be summarized in the more and more frequent designation of Mary as *coredemptrix*, "associate in redemption," a designation which occurs even in papal documents. It is these ideas of her cooperation in salvation which constitute the compelling motive behind the dogma of her immaculate conception. Only if she herself was without sin could she actively take part in the work of redemption. It is thus natural that Mary is continually designated as the prototype of the church, *Typus der Kirche*. Just as she is the mediatrix of all grace and the one through whom man comes to Christ, so one comes to Christ and participates in the divine grace through the church and its ministry. Mary, free from sin and mediatrix of all grace, becomes in the last analysis a personification of the church which is infallible and mediates all grace. Mariology is not an incidental outgrowth in Roman theology. It is a clear consequence of its conception of the church and the ministry, and therefore also of its view of the meaning of redemption. In the final analysis the Marian dogmas are a dogmatizing of the Roman church's understanding of herself. If we reject them, we must also reject the conception of the ministry expressed in the idea of representation.

Christology and the Evangelical Conception of the Ministry

After this excursus we now return to the evangelical point of view and ask on what basis we can claim that in the proclamation of the church, in its word and sacraments, we hear and meet Christ himself. In order to answer this question we may examine more closely the way in which the Lutheran confessions use the word in Luke 10:16, "He who hears you hears me," to which we alluded at the beginning of this section without giving it further consideration.

In doing so we find the same situation as encountered previously, namely, that here everything revolves around *the gospel* and not around the ministry as such. This gospel is in essence a word of forgiveness, and in the absolution it is therefore "the true voice of the Gospel" that is heard.[12] *Through this word* God truly makes men alive, and *therefore* it is to be believed as a word from heaven, because he who hears the gospel hears Christ himself. The church's power of the keys is clearly taken to be nothing else than the gospel itself operating in various forms, and therefore "this power is exercised only by teaching or preaching the Gospel and by administering the sacraments either to many or to individuals."[13] In order that the gift of the gospel may be offered to men "the ministry of the word and the sacraments" has been instituted. When the incumbent of the

[12] Apology of the Augsburg Confession, Article XII. *The Book of Concord, op. cit.*, p. 187.
[13] The Augsburg Confession, Article XXVIII. *Ibid.*, p. 82.

ministry performs this task of preaching the gospel, then "churches are therefore bound by divine law to be obedient to the bishops according to the text, 'He who hears you hears me.' "[14] But this obligation to obey is not unconditional. It is not obedience to the ministry as such, but obedience to the gospel. Consequently the quoted text continues, "However, when bishops teach or ordain anything contrary to the Gospel, churches have a command of God that forbids obedience. . . ."[15] The ministry exists for the sake of the gospel, and is therefore itself subordinate to it.

This conception is clearly expressed in the statements in the Apology of the Augsburg Confession which speak in terms rather similar to those used in Roman theology and declare that those who have been called to the ministry "do not represent their own persons but the person of Christ, because of the church's call, as Christ testifies (Luke 10:16), 'He who hears you hears me.' When they offer the Word of Christ or the sacraments, they do so in Christ's place and stead."[16] In addition it is stated that "the sacraments are efficacious even when evil men administer them, for ministers act in Christ's stead and do not represent their own persons, according to the word (Luke 10:16), 'He who hears you hears me.' "[17] The effectiveness of the gospel cannot be nullified by the hypocrisy of the ministers as long as they offer "the Word of Christ

[14] *Ibid.*, p. 84.
[15] *Ibid.*
[16] Apology of the Augsburg Confession, Articles VII and VIII. *Ibid.*, p. 173.
[17] *Ibid.*, p. 177.

or the sacraments." When they do this "because of the church's call," which is the call of Christ himself, they are the mouth of Christ and the hand of Christ. They speak and act on behalf of Christ. But this is valid only as long as they proclaim the gospel in truth and purity: "We should forsake wicked teachers because they no longer function in the place of Christ, but are antichrists."[18] Here the Apology quotes Paul's words in Galatians 1:9: "If anyone is preaching to you a gospel contrary to that which you received, let him be accursed." The efficacy of the gospel is independent of every special quality of the minister, whether his good or evil conduct, or his possession or lack of a special priestly grace conferred upon him by ordination. It is characteristic that, when the confessions discuss the efficacy of the word and the sacraments when they are administered by hypocrites, they make *no* reference to that which in any Roman Catholic discussion is of paramount importance, viz., the indelible character given through ordination, which renders the priest's ministerial acts valid and efficacious. The gospel does not possess its power and effect because it is proclaimed by an ordained minister, but because it is the gospel and thus also the voice of Christ himself in the church. "For Christ requires them to teach in such a way that he might be heard, because he says, '[he] hears me.'"[19] The decisive point here is not *who* speaks and acts, but *what* is said and done; for Christ's presence is not a presence in the ministerial office

[18] *Ibid.*
[19] Apology of the Augsburg Confession, Article XXVIII. *Ibid.*, p. 284.

as such, but in the various forms of the gospel.

What this means more exactly can be made clear through an example which corresponds to a central point in our previous presentation of the Roman point of view, namely the doctrine of the Lord's Supper. In the Lord's Supper Christ himself, his body and blood, are present, but "no man's work nor the recitation of the minister effect this presence of the body and blood of Christ in the Holy Supper, but it is to be ascribed solely and alone to the almighty power of our Lord Jesus Christ."[20] We have to do here with a presence by virtue of the word, not by virtue of the ministerial office. "For the truthful and almighty words of Jesus Christ which he spoke in the first institution were not only efficacious in the first Supper but they still retain their validity and efficacious power in all places where the Supper is observed according to Christ's institution and where his words are used, and the body and blood of Christ are truly present, distributed, and received by the virtue and potency of the same words which Christ spoke in the first Supper."[21] Here too when the Lord's Supper is celebrated according to the institution of Christ, and his words are heard, the minister acts on behalf of Christ, but not in order to offer Christ as a sacrifice to God, but in order to offer and impart him to the congregation. Christ comes *to us* in the Holy Supper. He does not come to be given to God as an act *by us*, but he comes as *God's* act

[20] Formula of Concord, Epitome, Article VII. *Ibid.*, p. 482.
[21] Formula of Concord, Solid Declaration, Article VII. *Ibid.*, p. 583.

and gift, the sacrifice of his overflowing love, which
is offered *to us*. The minister has here no "power"
over Christ. He is only a servant, a servant of the
word. This word is effective, not because it is the
minister's word, but because it is *the word of Christ*.

In this context, therefore, we find no emphasis
on the decisive redemptive significance of ordination and a valid succession, which characterizes
Roman theology. The writers of the confessions,
in answering the objections of their opponents concerning ordination, point out that it is "our deep
desire to maintain the church polity and various
ranks of the ecclesiastical hierarchy, although they
were created by human authority. We know that
the Fathers had good and useful reasons for insti-
tuting ecclesiastical discipline in the manner
described by the ancient canons."[22] But when the
bishops turn out to be "enemies of the Gospel" and
therefore are "unwilling to administer ordination,"
the congregation itself calls, chooses and ordains
men to be ministers of the word.[23] The ministry
exists in order that the gospel shall function, and
it derives its power and authority from this gospel
and not vice versa: "Nor is this ministry valid
because of any individual's authority but because
of the Word given by Christ."[24] If the bishops
want to serve the gospel, they will be retained in
accordance with good and ancient order, but the
power and efficacy of the gospel does not depend

[22] Apology of the Augsburg Confession, Article XIV. *Ibid.*,
p. 214.

[23] Treatise on the Power and Primacy of the Pope. *Ibid.*,
p. 331.

[24] *Ibid.*, p. 324.

on its being proclaimed by bishops.

If ordination is understood as being applicable to the ministry of the word, then "we have no objection to calling ordination a sacrament," because "God approves this ministry and is present in it."[25] The ministry is ordained by God, and all the "glorious promises" which speak of the power and efficacy of *the gospel* and *the word* (here the confessions refer to Romans 1:16 and Isaiah 55:11) apply to the preaching and administration of the sacraments by the ministry. It is this word in which Christ himself is present and active that creates faith, and *therefore* the ministry is necessary and given "highest praise."[26] That the ministry is necessary does not mean that it is "an effective means of salvation," as in the Roman conception, but it is necessary in order that the word of God, the gospel derived from Scripture, "may go forth and be proclaimed." In this case it is the word, not the ministry, that is "an effective means of salvation."

We note further that there is no suggestion that the activity of the ministry is a continuation or a completion of the redemptive work of Christ. This is due to the fact that we seek in vain for statements about the kind of "cooperation" between the divine and the human which characterizes the Roman conception. Such a line of thought is wanting, not only because it would mean a denial of the gospel itself with its judgment upon all our

[25] Apology of the Augsburg Confession, Article XIII. *Ibid.*, p. 212.
[26] Apology of the Augsburg Confession, Article IV. *Ibid.*, p. 117.

work and our righteousness and a denial, too, of the recreating gift of the life and righteousness of Christ, but also because it would be contrary to that view of the incarnation and the work of Christ which we find in the Christology of Luther, and which Roman theology rejects.

The Roman criticism was that Luther "underestimated" the humanity of Christ. This is a natural conclusion, if we search in his writings for statements about the human nature of Christ as something parallel to the divine nature and exercising its own redemptive activity. Such statements are not found in Luther. But we find a mass of statements about that which is of most decisive importance, that Christ was really human just as we are. It is not at all true that the humanity of Christ has lost its significance for Luther. No one has so intensively directed faith to the child in the manger and to the suffering man on the cross. But he does this precisely because in these very human situations he finds God himself. Here the ultimate issue is not a parallelism between the divine and the human, but a unified view of the divine and the human. Christ is even said to be human to a much greater degree than we are, in view of the fact that no one has so completely assumed the conditions of sinful man and made them his own, as when he submitted to the curse of the law and the agony of death. But precisely in this situation he proves that he is really true God, because none other than God could do this and conquer all the destructive powers of the enemy. The miracle of the incarnation and likewise of redemption is that

God himself is revealed in that which is most deeply human: in lowliness, service, and surrender to death. Here the wrath of God against sin and his love for the sinner are simultaneously revealed. Here we have in reality "God *in* Christ," and not a work accomplished by the human nature of Christ with the assistance of the divine. Christ's work as man is altogether God's own act, and for Luther the whole gospel depends on this very fact. And here we must note that which in the context of our discussion is the most decisive point. Just because *the deed of Christ as man* is at the same time also *God's own act*, this deed cannot be continued or completed *by men*. There is no need of such an "extension," because "it is finished." If in spite of this, one posits such an extension, it means that ultimately one trusts in his own works and not in the act of God in Christ, no matter how broadly one asserts that these works can be done only with the assistance of grace.

It would seem that there is no basis for the continually repeated charge in Roman theology that the evangelical view of the church and its ministry is a result of not taking the incarnation seriously. On the contrary it seems that the conception of the ministry suggested above on the basis of quotations from the confessions depends on the fact that the Lutherans have sought to take seriously that God in Christ "for us men and for our salvation" really "was made man," to use a statement from the Nicene Creed. Precisely in this confession of faith in Christ, common to both sides, do the paths diverge, even as they diverged at the

point of our common confession of the Spirit as
"Lord and Giver of life."

Christ's act of redemption as an act of God is
finished once for all, and it cannot be continued
and completed *by us*. On the contrary, it is necessary that Christ through his gospel comes *to us*
with all that he has secured—and this is the task
that belongs to the ministry of the church. That
which from the Roman conception of the meaning
of salvation appears as the *necessary* function of
the ministry, becomes from the Lutheran point of
view an *impossibility* and in the last analysis an
expression of that false way of salvation, where
ultimately one expects his salvation from his own
works and not from "Christ alone."

We have now seen that in the new ecumenical
situation with its initially confusing picture of
similar statements and apparently converging in-
terests we nevertheless at point after point can
discern a decisive difference between "Roman" and
"evangelical" thinking. And it turns out to be
essentially the same difference now as in the days
of the Reformation. Now as well as then it is in
the last analysis a question about the gospel of
justification, even if the antitheses now appear in
the form of questions which then were not central,
for instance in the form of Marian dogmas which
were not present in the days of the Reformation.

The decisive focus of today's problem turns out
to be exactly the relationship between "the word
and the church," or, more closely defined, the
relationship between the gospel of salvation and

the ministry of the church. Either salvation is provided through the ministerial office, and therefore word and sacraments are provided, the presence of Christ being dependent on his presence in the bearer of the office, or else salvation comes through the gospel in word and sacrament, and on this account there is a ministry in the church. The presence of Christ in the ministerial office is then dependent on the primary presence of Christ in the gospel itself.

The new situation demands a renewed and clear consideration on the basis of the gospel of those arguments which are propounded, not least in view of the current ecumenical discussion. We must not forget what it was that the Reformers and also the framers of the Protestant confessions of faith, on the basis of an intense study of the biblical texts, found to be that "chief article" by which the church stands and falls, *articulus stantis et cadentis Ecclesiae*. This article was not the ministerial office, nor even the scriptural principle as such, but it was the gospel of justification by grace through faith alone in Christ. It is an ominous sign when an evangelical church ceases to be concerned with the meaning of this gospel for the situation of modern man today, and instead tends to regard the question of the valid ministry and its form as that by which the church stands and falls.

INDEX

Type, 11 on 14 Waverly
Display, Baskerville
Paper, Standard R Antique